P9-EAN-976

Donald Hall

THE TOWN OF HILL

DAVID R. GODINE

BOSTON

David R. Godine, Publisher
Boston, Massachusetts

Copyright © 1971, 1972, 1973, 1974, 1975 by Donald Hall

LCC 74-25959
ISBN 0-87923-126-2
Printed in the United States of America

Acknowledgments:'To a Waterfowl' and 'The Town of Hill' first appeared in *American Poetry Review*. 'The Raisin' first appeared in *The New Yorker*. Other poems were originally published in *Ann Arbor Review*, *The Atlantic Monthly*, *Harper's Magazine*, *Hot Apples*, *Ironwood*, *Kayak*, *Lillabulero*, *Loon*, *Michigan Quarterly Review*, *The Ohio Review*, *Saturday Review*, *Stone Drum*, *Virginia Quarterly Review*, *The World*. Some of them also appeared as broadsides and postcards printed by The Red Hanrahan Press and Arts Workshop Press. Some were broadcast by the BBC.

A Godine Poetry Chapbook
Second Series

for Jane Kenyon

Contents

I   To a Waterfowl   10

The Presidentiad   12

Poem With One Fact   13

Professor Gratt   16

II   Fête   18

Jane at Pigall's   19

Breasts   20

Paper To Write On   21

Mouth   22

The Little Town   23

III   Lunch   26

Ballad of Goldenhair   27

Sudden Things   28

Transcontinent   29

I Lost My Overcoat in Omaha   30

The Space Spiders   32

Eleanor's Letters   34

The Brain Cells   35

IV   White Apples   38

The Green Shelf   39

The Raisin   40

Stories   42

A Poet at Twenty   43

The Town of Hill   44

The Town of Hill

To a Waterfowl

Women with hats like the rear ends of pink ducks
applauded you, my poems.
These are the women whose husbands I meet on
                                    airplanes,
who close their briefcases and ask, 'What are *you* in?'
I look in their eyes, I tell them I am in poetry,

and their eyes fill with anxiety, and with little tears.
'Oh, yeah?' they say, developing an interest in clouds.
'My wife, she likes that sort of thing? Hah-hah?
I guess maybe I'd better watch my grammar, huh?'
I leave them in airports, watching their grammar,

and take a limousine to the Women's Goodness Club
where I drink Harvey's Bristol Cream with their wives,
and eat chicken salad with capers, with little tomato
                                    wedges
and I read them 'The Erotic Crocodile,' and 'Eating You.'
Ah, when I have concluded the disbursement of
                                    sonorities,

crooning, 'High on thy thigh I cry, Hi!'—and so forth—
they spank their wide hands, they smile like Jell-O,
and they say, 'Hah-hah? My goodness, Mr. Hall,
but you certainly do have an imagination, huh?'
'Thank you, indeed,' I say; 'it brings in the bacon.'

But now, my poems, now I have returned to the motel,
returned to *l'éternel retour* of the Holiday Inn,
naked, lying on the bed, watching *Godzilla Sucks Mt. Fuji*,
addressing my poems, feeling superior, and drinking
                                                    bourbon
from a flask disguised to look like a transistor radio.

Ah, my poems, it is true,
that with the deepest gratitude and most serene pleasure,
and with hints that I am a sexual Thomas Alva Edison,
and not without collecting an exorbitant fee,
I have accepted the approbation of feathers.

And what about you? You, laughing? You, in the
                                                    bluejeans,
laughing at your mother who wears hats, and at your
                                                    father
who rides airplanes with a briefcase watching his
                                                    grammar?
Will you ever be old and dumb, like your creepy
                                                    parents?
Not you, not you, not you, not you, not you, not you.

11

The Presidentiad

Abraham Lincoln was giggling uncontrollably. Every few minutes he was able to stop for breath. Then he began giggling again. He had been giggling a hundred years. The strain showed terribly in his face. He was bent over, his knees nearly bumping his chin. He looked like a new mark of punctuation indicating uncontrollable laughter.

Washington sat with his thumb in his mouth.

Disraeli wore knickers and practiced swinging a golf club. He whistled frequently, which annoyed Calvin Coolidge, who had affected the dress of a Prussian general from the 1870 war. Occasionally one of us would see him pause before a mirror, but none of us took him seriously, nor the dwarf, who wore shorts and pretended to hunt butterflies.

Jefferson had not spoken since 1845. He appeared to have turned to stone, but regularly every three years a tear moved quickly from the corner of his left eye, and entered his beard, which had grown in 1911, where it evaporated. Several of us speculated that the tear was actually atmospheric, a periodic effect of condensation. But observation confirmed that the tear originated as the secretion of one duct.

The real weeper, however, was Ulysses S. Grant, who wept as continually and uncontrollably as Lincoln giggled. His face was purple, and invariably wet, and he surrounded himself with wet and drying handkerchiefs, which he used in a system of rotation.

Poem With One Fact

'At pet stores in Detroit, you can buy
frozen rats
for seventy-five cents apiece, to feed
your pet boa constrictor'
back home in Grosse Pointe,
or in Grosse Pointe Park,

while the free nation of rats
in Detroit emerges
from alleys behind pet shops, from cellars
and junked cars, and gathers
to flow at twilight
like a river the color of pavement,

and crawls over bedrooms and groceries
and through broken
school windows to eat the crayon
from drawings of rats—
and no one in Detroit understands
how rats are delicious in Dearborn.

If only we could *communicate*, if only
the boa constrictors of Southfield
would slither down I-94,
turn north on the Lodge Expressway,
and head for Eighth Street, to eat
out for a change. Instead, tomorrow,

a man from Birmingham enters
a pet shop in Detroit
to buy a frozen German Shepherd
for six dollars and fifty cents
to feed his pet cheetah,
guarding the compound at home;

and a woman from Bloomfield Hills,
with a refrigerated Buick
wagon, buys
a frozen police department Morgan
for thirty-seven dollars
for her daughter who loves horses.

Oh, they arrive all day, in their
locked cars, buying
schoolyards, bridges, buses,
churches, and Ethnic Festivals;
they buy a frozen Texaco station
for eighty-four dollars and fifty cents

to feed to an imported London taxi
in Huntington Woods;
they buy Tiger Stadium,
frozen, to feed to the Little League
in Grosse Ile;
they buy J. L. Hudson's, the Fisher Building,

14

the Chrysler Freeway, the Detroit Institute
of the Arts, Greektown,
Cobo Hall, and the Tri-City
Bucks Roller Derby
Team. They bring everything home,
frozen solid

as pig iron, to the six-car garages
of Harper Woods, Grosse Pointe Woods,
Farmington, Grosse Pointe
Farms, Troy, and Grosse Arbor—
and they ingest
everything, and fall asleep, and lie

coiled in the sun, while the city
thaws in the stomach and slides
to the small intestine, where enzymes
break down molecules of protein
to amino acids, which enter
the cold bloodstream.

Professor Gratt

And why does Gratt teach English? Why, because
A law school felt he could not learn the laws.
'Hamlet,' he tells his students, 'you will find,
Concerns a man who can't make up his mind.
The Tempest? . . . um . . . the one with Ariel! . . .
Are there more questions now?' But one can tell
That all his will, brains, and imagination
Are concentrated on a higher station:
He wants to be in the Administration.
Sometimes at parties he observes the Dean;
He giggles, coughs, and turns aquamarine.
Yet some day we will hear of 'Mr. Gratt,
Vice-President in Charge of This or That.'
I heard the Dean remark, at tea and cakes,
Face stuffed and sneering, 'Gratt has what it takes.'

II

Fête

Festival lights go on
in villages throughout
    the province, from Toe
Harbor, past the
    Elbow Lakes, to Eyelid Hill
when you touch me, there.

18

Jane at Pigall's

It is impossible to comprehend this *aubergine* that strays over her tongue looking for a rainbow. She wants to bang on the table.

This *Hollandaise* is matter that dissolves the material world. She wants to take off her clothes and embrace the plate.

The intensity of this veal *belle meunière*, in cooperation with a *Ch. d'Arche-Lafaurie* '61, transforms her body momentarily into vapor.

The vapor inhabits the entire restaurant, causing drug experiences among executives of the Kroger, Proctor and Gamble, and Baldwin Piano companies.

Stop it!, Jane screams. Nothing like this can really be happening! I must be asleep in Ann Arbor, dreaming of Pigall's in Cincinnati!

Breasts

Therc is something between us.

Paper To Write On

covered with lions
and smooth hair

granite of sleep
whispering baseball

master and owl
in wooden hayfields

gathering bees
horses and puzzles

ascending terrace
of Cincinnati

hunter of lapis
and smooth hair

Mouth

your mouth
is a garden in Arabia it is raining

I enter the mountain
under cheekbones like glaciers

your mouth is an old woman weaving
the same blanket

your mouth sits in the sun
dozing, but the fingers of your mouth
weave

birds migrate inside your mouth

when the birds reach the south plain
they are under the mountain

they waken the old woman
who feeds them the crumb of a yarn

Arabia! Arabia! Arabia!

The Little Town

I walk for a long time. These mountains are soft, and these valleys. Suddenly the skin of a mountain moves, and it becomes a valley. It's been raining here. New streams trickle through underbrush, among blue wildflowers, and butterflies as blue as the flowers they suck on.

Day after day, I keep walking. I realize that I am looking for something in particular. One day, I feel ready to find it. There is a faint sound, like a band playing. Kneeling down, my eyes close to a tuft of grass, I find a little town, as small as a pea; so small that the breath of a fern could blow it over.

In the town, people are having a parade. A band marches. Fat drummers in blue coats with white sashes bang drums. Cymbals clang. Trumpets toot. Dogs dance at the roadsides. Children jump and shout. How the marchers strut, puffing their chests out!

Then everything stops. Darkness. I lose the town in the grass. I cannot find it any more, so I lean back and close my eyes. In order to sleep, I tell myself stories:

'In the town, the children are falling asleep, under quilts patched from the dresses of their great-grandmothers. Their beds are soft with the down of geese that honked in these barnyards a hundred years ago. Dogs roll in their sleep, remembering slide trombones. The big drum roosts on a trestle in a barn.

'In their wide beds, the marchers and strutting tuba players dream about the old times, when the Emperor's lieutenants faded like newspapers left under snow, and they were free, and for the first time ever, danced and paraded in the streets of the little town.'

III

Lunch

It is necessary
 to make lunch for the children.

The arrow only moves
 to the target by halves.

Scheherezade seems unable
 to end a story.

Suicide is the target
 that recedes as I bend the bow.

Hold it!, I say, delayed
 by details of my quiver.

26

Ballad of Goldenhair

They enter the castle together,
   Goldenhair, Goldenhair,
In the sunlight, in fortunate weather,
And a drawbridge sequesters them there
In the down of the swan and the feather,
   O Goldenhair.

They remove their brocade and their lace,
   Goldenhair, Goldenhair,
And they lie under silk to embrace,
And no clock ever quarters the air
As he looks in the luminous face
   Of Goldenhair.

When he wakes she is standing alone,
   Goldenhair, Goldenhair,
Turned away, and as silent as stone,
Where mirrors recede pair by pair
Through darkening noon to the bone
   Of Goldenhair.

He approaches. She turns. She is dead,
   Goldenhair, Goldenhair,
And the skin of her cheek is a shred,
And she motions his bones to repair
To the jaws of the canopied bed,
   O Goldenhair.

Sudden Things

A storm was coming, that was why it was dark. The wind was blowing the fronds of the palm trees off. They were maples. I looked out the window across the big lawn. The house was huge, full of children and old people. Suddenly, as I looked into the ferns and the zinnias, I saw that the lion was loose!

Either because of the wind, or by malevolent human energy, which is the same thing, the cage had come open. Suppose a child walked outside! A child walked outside. I knew that I must protect him from the lion. I threw myself on top of the child. The lion roared over me. Suddenly, there was a loud cracking noise in the branches and the bushes. The lion cringed back in terror. I looked up and saw that the elephant was loose!

The elephant was taller than the redwoods. He was hairy like a mammoth. His tusks trailed vines. Parrots screeched around his head. His eyes rolled crazily. He trumpeted: the ice-cap was breaking up!

The lion backed off, whining. The boy ran for the house. I covered his retreat. I locked all the doors, and pulled the bars across them. An old lady tried to open a door to get a better look. I spoke sharply to her. She sat down grumbling and pulled the blanket over her knees.

Out of the window I saw zebras and rattlesnakes and wildebeests and cougars and woodchucks on the lawns and in the tennis courts. I worried how, after the storm, we would put the animals back in their cages, and get to the mainland.

Transcontinent

Where the cities end, the
dumps grow the oil-can shacks,
from Portland, Maine,

to Seattle. Broken
cars rust in Troy, New York,
and Cleveland Heights.

On the train, the people
eat candy bars, and watch,
or fall asleep.

When they look outside and
see cars and shacks, they know
they're nearly there.

I Lost My Overcoat in Omaha

A scarf resides
at the Fifth Avenue Hotel.
It is frail, at such an age.
On a cool
day of summer, it walks
in Washington Square, early,
before
'the young people come.'

At the bottom of an elevator shaft
at the Drake in Chicago
there is the shadow
of a tweed jacket. It
does sums, over
and over, like a museum director.
It has hidden
successfully.

Shirt, trousers, and one
pair of underpants
take breakfast and lunch
on the nineteenth floor
of the Fairmont, in San Francisco,
directly over a red
waterhole
outside Milledgeville, Georgia.

On the road from Carmel
to Big Sur, glinting
in the sun that never goes down
—like a penny, like a new
Chevrolet, like a cellophane
cake package—
the suit of skin I lost there
hitches a ride.

The Space Spiders

All autumn and into winter they attacked the mother ship. The diameter of each of their bodies was a hundred thousand miles. Each of them had a hundred thousand legs which moved slowly and never stopped. The hairs that grew from their legs were the size of oil cars.

A hundred thousand space spiders attacked the mother ship. I was outside polishing the surface. In the shiny metal I saw the stars disappear, as the patches of blackness moved closer. Quickly, I accelerated to the spacedeck, entered, and swung the thick door shut, as the first legs felt for it.

I extended the metal lids over the portholes. I turned out the spacelights, and sat in the darkness at the center of the ship. I found that my breath was quietest if I placed my head between my knees and ankles.

Outside, I heard them whine and buffet against the smooth white sides.

✻　✻　✻

After a long time the noises stopped. I opened a porthole a little. If I had seen a hair that grew from the hair of a leg, I would have gone back to the darkness.

I went outside again. With my electron telescope, I scanned the air: in the outermost nebula, a million light years away, I saw small circles of blackness crawling like crabs on a beach. I went back to polishing the surface, but frequently glanced at the reflection of the void behind me.

That was years ago.

Now I have retired to Centerville. It is pleasant here, walking to the post office and sitting in the park under the oak trees, on the days when it does not rain. Not to mention the Carnegie Library; not to mention Smitty's Drugstore; not to mention the widows, who mostly keep to themselves, doing the same jigsaw puzzles year after year.

Eleanor's Letters

I who picked up the neat
Old letters never knew
The last names to complete
'Aunt Eleanor' or 'Lew.'

She talked about the weather,
And canning, and a trip
Which they might take together
'If we don't lose our grip.'

But 'Lew has got a growth
Which might turn out, they say,
Benign, or shrink, or both.'
Then, 'Lewis passed away.'

He didn't *die*. That word
Seemed harsh and arbitrary
And thus was not preferred
In her vocabulary.

'Everything's for the better,'
She wrote, and what is more,
She signed her dying letter
'As ever, Eleanor.'

The Brain Cells

Inside the brain they are holding a mass funeral for the dead brain cells.

Survivors stand like poplars at the side of *l'avenue George Cinq.* Gray rain. The brain cells carry umbrellas which are also gray. The funeral cortège is eighty miles long. All day, from ten in the morning until seven in the evening, the procession hauls its body along the avenue.

It is June first, 1972. On the night of May thirty-first, the dikes burst, strangling and dragging away the citizens.

Muted drums beat slowly.

Black horses wearing black plumes draw black carriages and caissons past the viewing stand draped with mourning where the President, the Prime Minister, members of the Cabinet, and leading Senators stand all day in their black suits with black armbands, hands over their hearts.

Trumpets play death music. Newspapers bordered with black announce:

MASS DISASTER FIVE BILLION DEAD

and newsboys walk slowly on the edge of the crowd.

As the long day slopes into night the last brain cell is buried. The brain cells, weary of marching, grave-digging, and standing in the rain all day, walk homeward

35

slowly to their gray apartments off Battleship Potempkin Square. They switch on their hotplates and make themselves bouillon.

Then they sit back on their tatty sofas, turn on the TV, and watch the replays, in black and white, over and over.

IV

White Apples

when my father had been dead a week
I woke
with his voice in my ear
                          I sat up in bed
and held my breath
and stared at the pale closed door

white apples and the taste of stone

if he called again
I would put on my coat and galoshes

The Green Shelf

Driving back from the market,
bags of groceries beside me,
I saw on a lawn
the body of a gray-haired man
twisted beside his power mower.

A woman twisted
her hands above him, mouth wide
with a cry.
She bent close to him, straightened,
bent again, straightened,

and an ambulance
stopped at the curb.
I drove past them slowly
while helpers
kneeled by the man.

Over the stretcher
the lawnmower continued to throb
and absently
the hand of the old woman
caressed the shuddering

handle. Back,
I put the soupcans in order
on the green shelves,
pickles, canned milk, peas,
basil and tarragon.

The Raisin

I drank cool water from the fountain
in the undertaker's parlor
near the body of a ninety-two-year-old man.

Harry loved horses and work.
He curried the flanks of his Morgan,
he loaded crates twelve hours—to fill in
when his foreman got drunk—
never kicking a horse,
never kind to a son.

He sobbed on the sofa ten years ago,
when Sally died.
We heard of him dancing
with widows in Florida, cheek
to cheek, and of scented
letters that came to Connecticut
all summer.

When he was old he made up for the weeping
he failed to do earlier—
grandchildren, zinnias,
Morgans, great-grandchildren—
he wept over everything. His only
advice. 'Keep your health.'
He told old stories, laughing slowly.
He sang old songs.

Forty years ago his son
who was parked making love in the country
noticed Harry parked making love
in a car up ahead.

When he was ninety he wanted to die.
He couldn't ride or grow flowers
or dance
or tend the plots in the graveyard
that he had kept up
faithfully, since Sally died.

This morning I looked into the pale
raisin of Harry's face.

Stories

I look at the rock and the house;
I look at the boat on the river;
I sit on the colored stone
and listen to stories:

the mountain shudders
at the breath of a lizard
and the stream disappears
in a tunnel of jewels;

the walk of a woman
into darkness stops
when a snake hisses
with the voice of a cavern;

when the rock turns to air
the sun touches
her body, and diamonds
and the talking lake:

cool air at noon,
light on deep water,
fire at night
in the squares of the winter.

A Poet at Twenty

Images leap with him from branch to branch. His eyes brighten, his head cocks, he pauses under a green bough, alert.

And when I see him I want to hide him somewhere.

The other wood is past the hill. But he will enter it, and find the particular maple. He will walk through the door of the maple, and his arms will pull out of their sockets, and the blood will bubble from his mouth, his ears, his penis, and his nostrils. His body will rot. His body will dry in ropey tatters. Maybe he will grow his body again, three years later. Maybe he won't.

There is nothing to do, to keep this from happening.

It occurs to me that the greatest gentleness would put a bullet into his bright eye. And when I look in his eye, it is not his eye that I see.

The Town of Hill

Back of the dam, under
a flat pad

of water, church
bells ring

in the ears of lilies,
a child's swing

curls in the current
of a yard, horned

pout sleep
in a green

mailbox, and
a boy walks

from a screened
porch beneath

the man-shaped
leaves of an oak

down the street looking
at the town

of Hill that water
covered forty

years ago,
and the screen

door shuts
under dream water.